Motivated for Greatness

To Mr. [name]

Thank you for your leadership and your love. May God Bless You.

Arletta L. Moore

Motivated for Greatness
7 Steps to Mastering Your Greatness

Arletta L. Moore

Arletta L. Moore

Publishing Information

Motivated for Greatness
7 Steps to Mastering Your Greatness

Copyright © 2016 by Arletta L. Moore
All rights reserved.

Book cover design by LaShawn Chandler of D'Vine Design www.lashawnchandler.com

Photography by kimphotography.com

This book is dedicated to my Mom.

Thank you for choosing me.

Thank you for loving me.

And, thank you for giving me a new life.

Arletta L. Moore

Table of Contents

Acknowledgements 9

Introduction 14

Chapter 1: Greatness is as Greatness Does 17

Chapter 2: My Life, My Life, My Life.................................. 22

Chapter 3 Step 1: Connecting with God............................. 51

Chapter 4 Step 2: Dig up the roots...................................... 59

Chapter 5: Step 3 - Get Rid of the Baggage 74

Chapter 6: Step 4 - Stop the People Pleasing...................... 80

Chapter 7: Step 5 - Change your mindset.......................... 85

Chapter 8: Step 6 - Love Yourself More............................. 91

Chapter 9: Step 7 - Live your Dreams................................. 98

Chapter 10: Getting through the rough times 103

Chapter 11: Time to celebrate your mastery of greatness .. 107

Conclusion 111

For booking inquiries 113

Arletta L. Moore

Acknowledgements

To My Lord and Savior, Jesus Christ:

My entire life has been a journey for me, and there has been some good times and bad times, but I would not be the person I am today without the people that had such an impact on my life. I want to first give honor to my Lord and Savior, Jesus Christ. I knew as a young child the power of prayer. At that time, I made Jesus the head of my life. Thank you Jesus, for seeing the greatness within me, even when I didn't see it in myself.

To my loving, caring, and supportive family:

I'm so happy to have ALL of you in my life. There used to be a time when I felt like it was me against the world, but now my family is bigger than I ever could have imagined, and I thank you all your love and support. I love each of you.

Arletta L. Moore

To my mother, Shirley Nolen:

    I dedicate this book to you because you chose me. If it weren't for you, I don't know where I would be today. I thank you for your love and the lessons you have taught me about being a woman. You are the epitome of a strong black woman, and your strength is what I admire the most about you.

To my sisters Porsche Pope and Twanisha Glass:

    You two are my very best friends and I love both of you for the support you have given to me throughout this journey. Porsche, we talked almost every day during this process and your encouraging words was just what I needed to push me forward, when I wanted to give up. Twanisha, you and I had an interesting beginning, but I can tell you that we are closer now than we have ever been before. You have always been my protector and my defender, and your love proves that you will always support me no matter what. I thank you for always being my cheerleader.

To my closes friends, Kenya Simmons and Tina Moore:

I appreciate you all so much for always being there and always giving me encouraging words of wisdom. Kenya you have been my rock for years and you have pushed me to limits, I didn't know I could reach. Tina, your help with this manuscript assist me to understand what was needed to make this one of my best work. Also no matter what I do, I know I can always count on you for support. I love you both from the bottom of my heart.

To my biological family:

It's been 13 years since we have reconnected and although developing the relationship has been a slow process, I'm happy that we have started to build a connection together again. Our journey together is what inspired me to write this book.

Arletta L. Moore

To my mentor and Business Coach, Millie Lee:

    WOW, you lit the fire in me and because of that, my dream to become an author has come true. The many days and nights we spent to make sure this manuscript was perfect, meant so much to me. I can't thank you enough for believing, motivating and encouraging me. Thank God for your spirit, your love, and your friendship.

Last but certainly not least, to my dear husband, Gerald Moore:

    Thank you so much for believing in me and believing in my vision. You are the one that took this leap of faith with me on this journey and I can't thank you enough for trusting me. Thank you for your love and support. I love you always.

Motivated for Greatness

Introduction

"If you want to grow and develop yourself, embrace failure. If you want to become the best at what you do, you've got to be willing to fail, again and again. And then finally, one day, you can fail your way to greatness."

~ Les Brown

Sometimes life takes us on an emotional roller coaster and we don't understand why and we are not sure how to handle it. Motivated for greatness is about the journey I had to face throughout my life, and although there were some hard times, I managed to find the greatness within me. I was inspired by Les Brown, one of my favorite motivational speakers. He wrote a book called, "You Have Greatness Within You". A couple years ago I read this book and it encouraged me to take a leap of faith into my greatness by the powerful words he wrote in that book. It took me a long time for to acknowledge the greatness in my own life. There were times in my life that I struggled with embracing the significance within me due to my past. I knew I needed to make a change in my life, because I knew God had a bigger plan for my life, and it was bigger than what I predicted for my own self. I thought I had to rely on my own ability, but I had to listen to the spirit that was guiding me to God's purpose which also led me into greatness.

Writing this book was challenge for me, as I had to go back to a very dark place in my life, that I had not visited in a long time. However, there was a mandate on my life to release the wounds and share the steps I took to move me from the gutter of despair to greatness. Therefore, if you feel stuck and are tired of living a mediocre life, then this book is for you! Now this book is twofold, the first part I reveal my life's story, so that you will understand what motivated me to write this book. On the other hand, this book will equip you with practical steps to assist you to transform your own life. Therefore, get ready to move beyond your past. No more self-doubt and fear, because today is a new day. Leap into the pages and grab a hold to the greatness that has been awaiting you.

Motivated for Greatness

Chapter 1

Greatness is as Greatness Does

"It is a rough road that leads to the heights of greatness."
~ Lucius Annaeus Seneca

What is Greatness? Merriam-Webster defines greatness as the quality of being great, distinguished, or eminent. Yet, how do we define greatness? Is greatness defined by the things we do, or how we have impacted the world in a positive way? There are people that have made the world the way it is through their personal bravery like, Nelson Mandela, Mother Teresa, and Gandhi. They are considered to be some of the world's greatest people to have ever lived. Then there are others who have shaped the way we think, like Albert Einstein, Plato or Martin Luther King Jr. Then there are those who inspired us because of their triumphant over adversities, like great athletes such as Michael Jordan and Serena

Williams, artists as Michelangelo and Gordon Parks, writers as Edgar Allan Poe and Langston Hughes, entrepreneurs as Madam CJ Walker and John H. Johnson, or inventors like Thomas Edison and George Washington Carver. Compared to these giants of mankind, our lives may seem a little insignificant. In fact, greatness is hidden within all of us, we just need the right opportunity or the right circumstance to nourish our full potential.

This is what I've learn from my past. I had to cognize that my greatness came in distinctive varieties, and the only way for me to understand it was for me to become fully myself and surpass my doubts and superficial limitations. Greatness doesn't mean that I needed to do huge things, it just meant that whatever I did, I needed to pour into my complete being.

Now let's take it a step further when we define greatness. Take a look at our passion, our passion is what gives us the strength to follow our dreams. It's the powerhouse that can uncover our hidden greatness, since passion drives us forward and allows us to overcome setbacks and obstacles. We are human, so failure, disappointment, hurts and making mistakes are inevitable, it's part of the process of getting us to our greatness. Nevertheless, we shouldn't allow the failed results of our past to diminish our excellence.

Look at how often toddlers fall over and over when they learn to walk. The reason many of us give up after initial problems is because failure seems to reinforce hidden self-doubts. We have to understand that in making mistakes we begin the process of learning. Even the pain we endure is all part of the process. A great example of us finding greatness within us is our failure rate. I know this sounds crazy, but each so-called failure we have overcome is a step towards actualizing our dream and reviling our greatness.

So you see, just like the many greats of the past, just because we have seen many setbacks, and challenges, it does not mean that we don't have greatness within us. It's time to discover what makes us great and embrace the brilliance that God has bless us with. Greatness is about not only lifting ourselves, but how we can uplift others through the growth from our pain. The next chapter is a treat. I shed a light into my life story to let you know how I overcame my despair of the past and moved into my greatness.

Arletta L. Moore

Chapter 2

My Life, My Life, My Life

"My life may not be going the way I planned it, but it is going exactly the way God planned it." ~Anonymous

When I was young, I didn't understand my purpose in life. I was raised in an abusive household, which led me to a life where I didn't feel accepted or have a sense of belonging. As a result, my identity was tainted because of the lack of love shown to me by my mother. For five years, this was my life. I often felt unwanted and unloved. I yearned to be accepted by those who were supposed to love me. I thought, if only I could make my mom happy, the physical abuse would stop.

Despite being young, I recall an instance when my mom left me home alone. In my continuing efforts to make her happy, I mean truly happy, I decided to cook a meal for her when she returned. I thought surely this would stop the physical abuse, and maybe even put a smile on her face. Consequently, I began to prepare the meal. As you can imagine at five years old, cooking was not my forte, so I turned the stove on too high and caused a fire that burned a hole in the wall.

The ambulance and fire trucks arrived, and since my mother wasn't home a neighbor came and safely removed me from the house. Upon her return, my mother was not at all happy about what had transpired. Instead of being happy, as I had hoped, she was so upset with me. I remember her yelling at me and then out of nowhere she punched me in my mouth.

I grabbed a hold of my mouth and started to cry really loud from the sheer pain and my hurt feelings. I remember the blood gushing from my mouth, and I ran to the bathroom to spit blood in the sink. My lips were swollen. They were so big; I could not close my mouth. As I was attempting to soothe myself, my mother entered the bathroom, snatched me, and took me into my room. Once in my room she told me to look into the mirror and look at my lips. Seeing my reflection cause a large amount of tears to stream down my face. I thought to myself, *what am I doing wrong?* At that moment, my mother said "This is what you get for burning a hole in the kitchen wall, and this will teach you not to do it again."

That night, as I laid in bed, I cried, not only because of the burning sensation from the salt my mother placed under my gums to ease my lip swelling but, as I didn't know what else to do. At that moment, I started to pray to God for His help: "God help me be a better girl so that mommy would love me more and stop beating me."

Despite my prayer, the abuse continued. I recall an instance when my mother overheard me cursing while playing with my dolls. As a result, of my upbringing I thought all communication and discipline involved cursing. So, when my dolls didn't do what I wanted I began cursing at them. I was the only child living with my mother, so my dolls were my only outlet of communication. When my mother overheard me she yelled, "You about to get your butt whooped. Now do you want the ironing cord or the extension cord!?!?" I instantly began to cry and plead with her not to beat me. Not directly answering the question seemed to only infuriate my mother and she decided to use the ironing cord and began to beat me furiously.

The next day, revealed scars on my arms and legs that remain to this day. I still struggled to understand why I was always in trouble. Especially since my daily purpose and goal was to avoid the constant abuse at all costs. I kept thinking the reason was simply that my mother didn't love me enough. I say enough because I assumed that like all parents my mother had to love me, but clearly she didn't love me enough to stop beating me. This was my life up to the age of five.

A few months later, my mother told me that I was going somewhere and I need to get dressed. After getting dressed, she sat me down at the kitchen table and started combing my hair. As she combed my hair, she started telling me about this "special" place. A special place, I was so excited to go to, since aside from school I was always in the house. This place must be really special because I was dressed in my best outfit and my hair was done.

It turns out this "special" place was an orphanage. I didn't know this at the time. I thought it was some type of camp for kids, but it wasn't. It was a place that is not synonymous with the words fun, exciting or "special". With only the clothes on my back, I ventured off to this "special" place. As I walked into this "special" place, I was greeted by a nice lady, who guided me down this long hallway. As I was walking down the hallway with this lady, I started to look around and I saw there were all these different kinds of rooms with children in them playing with toys. The rooms also had several beds, so then I started to I think to myself that this may not be a short trip. I also thought, "Why didn't my mommy come here with me?" The lady led me to the last room at the end of the hallway and said to me, "Well sweetie, here's your new room." My "new" room? I couldn't understand what she meant, because this was far from my mommy's house. I began to cry, and this is when I realized that I was going to be there for a while. I was there long enough to realize that I may not be going back home.

It was dark and cold, and I opted not to play with the many other children that were there. I cried daily because I longed to be back with my mother. Even though my home was abusive, at least I was with people I knew. After a few weeks at the orphanage, I remember meeting another nice lady, and she told me that I was going to a "new" place.

Hoping that unlike the orphanage this would

be the "special" place that my mother was referring to a few weeks back. As we drove away from the orphanage, I kept asking her if I was going to see my mother. She smiled and told me that it was going to be a surprise. After about 15 minutes of driving, we finally pulled up to a home that I didn't recognize. I yelled, "THIS IS NOT MY HOUSE!", and refused to get out the car. She asked me in the kindest voice I had ever heard, to come inside because there were cookies. As we walked toward the house, I saw another lady on the porch waiting for us. Once inside the house the lady greeted us. The woman in the house said to me, "Hi sweetie." All I could do is cry. I knew this was not my mother's home. It was at that moment, that I painfully realized I was not going home. The lady that brought me to this home, tried to get me to stop crying, and explained to me that this was my new home.

It was bad enough that I had to deal with the abuse in my biological home, now I had to face the fact that my mother did not want me anymore and sent me to this strange place. So here I am, five years old, and I go from living in an abusive and unloving home, to being shipped off to a very unfamiliar place. As I cried, I looked around and said, "Where is my mother?" The lady that drove to this "new place" happens to be my social worker, she told me that this was my new home, and I was not happy. I was confused, and I couldn't understand exactly what was happening.

I spent the next four years of my life in that "new place" aka foster home, and being there only made me feel guilty for being born and unwelcomed. This "new place" was even more torture. I was force to clean, cook and wash dishes. At the age of five, I was constantly told and reminded by my foster parents that I should be appreciative because I had a place to live and I had to be there because my mother didn't want me anymore. I tried to be grateful, but it was at a huge cost. I remember washing dishes so much that my arms broke out from the dishwashing liquid. Since I was so young and short, I had to use cutting boards to help me to reach the sink. As I washed the dishes, I laid my arms on the sink, which caused the breakout. One day at school, my teacher notice my arms and called me into the principal's office. My teacher asked me what happened, and I simply told her the truth that I was washing dishes at home. My teacher and the principal called my foster home and told them that they were concerned about the breakout on my arms and they couldn't understand why a five-year-old was washing dishes. My foster parents were not pleased that I had been discussing what happened in the home. When I got home, I was in big trouble. I encountered a beating and was told that what goes on in the house stays in the house, and I was not to tell anybody our business! I really felt bad about what happened, so that's when people pleasing began. I continued to do everything I possibly could to make sure that I pleased or found acceptance with my foster parents, but that didn't work. I was constantly in trouble and I could not understand why.

I remember being in school and my teacher kept telling me to stay in my seat, but I didn't. To restrain myself from getting out of my seat, I decided to put Elmer's glue in my seat. Of course, the teacher, realized what I had done, therefore I was in trouble, and this didn't sit well with my foster parents. I couldn't figure out how I was able to be that good little girl and not get in trouble all the time. Therefore, I prayed for God's help. Yes, still at a young age, I was still praying.

So here I am in another home trying to get understanding, love and acceptance from new people which was hard. I began to think that this was the life that God wanted me to have, and I had to deal with it accordingly. I stayed with my foster parents four years. I know four years isn't a long time, but my time there seemed like an eternity; a nightmare that just wouldn't end.

Looking back, I felt like I was a slave. I was made to clean the house. I also had to wash walls, clean the baseboards and instead of using a vacuum cleaner to clean the carpet, I had to pick up the lint with my hands. I couldn't watch TV, I couldn't play with the other foster kids, and if I got into trouble, I couldn't eat. I recall sometimes going days without eating.

All of the abuse in the foster home kept me in a daydream state of a better life. I can recall myself and another girl in the foster home sitting up late at night and talking about a life with our new adoptive family. Our foster mother constantly told us that our time at the foster home was not going to be long, for our stay there was just temporary. This gave us hope that we would be in loving homes with parents that would give us the world.

I can remember a day in early part of November of 1981, when a lady came to visit me at the foster home. I was playing in the basement with the other children, and my foster mother called me up stairs, so I could meet this lady. As my foster mother introduced us, she informed me that the lady that came to the house was in the process of adopting me. I was so excited. My foster mother told me that I would be spending the next couple of weekends with the woman who was interested in adopting me, so that I could meet and hangout with her and her daughter. This made my heart sing, because finally my prayers were answered. This was my chance to be in a loving home and gained a sister. For the next few weeks I spent time with my new mom and her daughter who eventually became my sister.

I was glad in 1982 when the adoption process was now complete. I was now in a loving home, and my life truly began. At least that was my perception. I can be me now, and not stuck under this rock shamed of where I came from.

Ok now that I was adopted, I could began living my life the way God had designed it to be.

However, as time went on, I continued with the people pleasing, insecurity, and low self-esteem. As complex as adoptions are, it still did not help me get over my issues. Throughout my elementary, middle, and high school years, I continued trying to please and be accepted by others.

I was so afraid of being myself that I became the shadow of my adoptive sister. I wanted her to accept me, so I did everything I possibly could to make sure I pleased her. This led me to becoming her doormat. She didn't realize it but she was my idol. In my eyes, she had the perfect life. She had parents that loved her, and a father that treated her like a princess. Everyone around us had this perception of my sister, and it was a little different than the perception they had of me. She was smart, pretty and everyone loved her. Me on the other hand, I was shy, quite and I didn't do very well in school.

There were times when I felt as if I was a charity case, like I was just this poor little girl that was adopted because of the abuse in her biological home. Now I'm not saying that my adoptive mother and my new family didn't love me, it's just that they had a special kind of love for my sister than they did for me. This is why I wanted her life.

I wanted my sister's looks, and her brains. I thought, if only I could just be like her, then my life would be perfect. I didn't realize that being her was not being me, and I had to learn to love myself and build my self-esteem. I just didn't know how to do it.

My sister and I used to fight a lot. When we were young, what she didn't know was I used to let her pick on me just so that I could have a connection with her. During our many fights, she would dig her nails in my hand so much that it would bleed and leave scars that I still have to this day. Since my self-esteem was stripped from me as a young child, I thought that I could find my identity through my sister. I would wear her clothes to school, and when she found out, I was in trouble. She just didn't understand that I want to be her and be accepted by her.

My sister was beautiful and everybody loved her. She had a great personality, and everyone wanted to be her friend. She was tall, light-skin and had this long beautiful hair. As for me, I was the total opposite. I was short, dark skin with a short Jeri-Curl, and I had large glasses that almost covered my entire face. Sometimes my Jeri-curl would look like an afro because it wasn't always maintained. Comparing myself to my sister only furthered my self-esteem's down a downward spiral.

I continued this behavior throughout elementary, middle, and high school. In elementary school, I was picked on and bullied. All I wanted was for people to like and accept me. Until I reached grade school, I never realized how mean kids could be sometimes and I didn't know how to defend myself, so I would just take the verbal abuse from my classmates.

I continued this behavior in college years and while working in Corporate America. It also spilled into my love life. I was trying to please every man I met. In college I would try and find some type of connection with a guy so that they would accept me. This led me to do things that I should not have done in order to be accepted in their eyes.

The things I did to please a man resulted in an abortion, a sexually transmitted disease and contemplating suicide. I was lowest point of my life. As cliché as this may sound, I was looking for love in all the wrong places.

This lead me to very promiscuous in my early 20's. I thought even the slightest interest from a guy meant he liked me and he would quickly consummate the relationship. There were many times when I felt disgusted with myself, like why would I put myself through this. Problem was; I didn't understand that I was looking for love outside of me. I couldn't find that love within myself. In my late 20's and early 30's, this unfilled desire to be loved was so overwhelming that I contemplated suicide. I did not know how to control or contain these thoughts. I thought maybe it wasn't meant for me to remain in this world. Deep down inside, I just wanted to know that God had a plan for my life, I just needed some answers and I needed them soon!

In my mind, I thought that if I had not aborted that child or if I had the man of my dreams, then God would reveal his plan for my life, and everything would be perfect. I also thought that if I didn't find my purpose soon, my life would come to an end. I was so tired of getting hurt and it was finally too much to handle.

After graduating from college with a degree in Electrical Engineering Technology, I stayed with my mom for about six months. Deep down inside I knew that I had to quickly find a job, and be on my own to begin to truly understand who I was. The first step was to relocate. There was too much pain for me in

Arletta L. Moore

Detroit.

In November of 1999, I was offered a job in Warren, Ohio and moved there in January of 2000. Although I was happy to be moving out of my mom's house and being on my own, there were still some things I had to face. I had to find my confidence and strengthen my low self-esteem to address my need to be loved.

While I was in Ohio, I found out that I was pregnant by a guy I had dated in college. Of course, he did not want the child nor me, so continuing my people pleasing, I aborting the child, consequently to stay connected with him. I never once took my own feelings into consideration. I knew this was what he wanted, so I made it happen. I went to the first abortion clinic I found to have the abortion. I later discovered that the abortion clinic I went to had some serious issues with how they ran the clinic and later was shut down by the state board.

After I had the abortion, it caused me to have an appendicitis. My breaking point was beginning, because I wasn't sure where life was taking me. Since I had the abortion, I thought the person I was dating would stay with me because I did what I thought would please him. Well I guessed wrong; later on that year, he told me that I wasn't his type and broke up with me. I was devastated because I had the abortion, and as a side effect an appendectomy because of the abortion. I cried for days, I couldn't figure out what was wrong with me, why didn't he love me or better yet, why didn't I love myself? Love myself enough to prevent me from even being in this situation. Looking for love in all the wrong places behavior continued for years. I continued to do this same behavior going from one "relationship" to the next, expecting different results.

Later that year I got into another relationship with someone who had me on cloud nine. I knew this was it, because he showed me so much attention and really cared about me. That relationship was short lived because he was already in a committed relationship. *If only I could get him to like me enough to leave his girlfriend, then things would be great,* so I thought. The relationship lasted for a year and because I was the "side chick", I had to wait my turn to spend time with him. I was okay with this position because I had such a good time with him and I love the way he made me feel when we were together.

He took real interest in me and wanted to do many things with me. We did so much together like going to the movies, dinner and hung out at the club. I can remember a time when we decide to call in sick from work, and go to the amusement park. This is the type of relationship that I was longing. I never felt this type of connection with a guy, and it felt so good. However, as you may know, that type of relationship never lasts. I soon realized that I needed to end this relationship. It was not good for me, and I had to make a change soon. I was tired of being the side chick, and I knew this was not the type of relationship God wanted me to have in my life. I went into prayer and cried out to God asking for His help. At that moment I knew. It was time to do what was right for me. I needed to end this quick. At that point I decided to make a change in my life. A change that involved putting me first.

Breaking it off with him was not easy, it hurt. I had to start doing things differently. I had to make some changes. When I took that leap of faith and ended the relationship, that's when I knew that some good things were going to happen, because I was making strides in the right way. Although this was the phase in the right course, I still had to undo over 20 years of damage.

As I was cleaning up my love life, I needed to clean up my career as well. I wasn't very confident in my ability to work at the company that hired me. Therefore, I exerted the minimal of effort just to get by, and the company knew that, so in 2002, I was laid off. This was probably best, because during that time, I was growing closer to God. He was showing me things in my life that were starting to give me a sense of direction.

Four months after getting laid-off, I landed a job in Fort Wayne, Indiana. I was sad and happy all at the same time when I received the news. First, I was sad because I was in another small city, where I didn't know anyone. Plus, I had no desire what so ever to live in Fort Wayne. Secondly, I was happy because now I had another opportunity to do better than I was doing in Warren, OH.

Despite the fact that I was happy about the new opportunity, it also came with some challenges. Not only challenges on the job, but challenges in my personal life. I really wanted things to work out at my new job in Fort Wayne, but I so was depressed. I was lonely and I knew that there was something I was longing for… and that was Love and connection. Maybe this was a false sense of love since I was depressed and lonely. My thought was if I had real and true Love then I could move past my loneliness.

So all while in Fort Wayne, I was chased love. Not realizing that God was really showing me that I had to love myself first, I was just oblivious to it at that time. I wanted to first get over this aloneness, and find a great connection with someone. My mindset was if only I found that person to love me, *then* I would love myself and didn't feel this emptiness inside of me. Nevertheless, with every chase for love, there was something pushing me further and further way from God and His purpose for me.

I stayed in a depressive state for 4 years. Many nights I cried so hard that I woke up with puffy eyes. I didn't want to do anything, but just stay in my apartment. This was also during the time Sex and the City series was out on DVD. I would sit in my apartment and watch hours of Sex and the City. I had to find a way to escape my pain and depression.

I also found that liquor help me mass the pain I was feeling about myself. One day I was so depressed with my life that I drank an entire bottle of tequila. Luckily in my drunkenness, called a close friend that lived near my apartment and I was trying to have a conversation with her. She couldn't understand me because I was slurring my words as I was trying to talk to her. That next moment I blanked out. I woke up in the emergency room.

I continued this emotional roller coaster until one-day God opened my eyes. It was February, 2007. God came to me in a vision and told me, "your story is going to help millions of people." I wasn't really sure what He meant by that, but I knew I had a story, but I did not know it would be able to help millions of people. My walk with God grew stronger, and as a result I decided to end a very toxic relationship. It was more toxic for me, because in the relationship it was made clear that he was not interested in having a committed relationship with me. He was only interested in having a friendship with benefits, but I was trying to have a real committed relationship with him. Although I was hurt, the relationship came to an end, and, God revealed to me that it was time for me to put me first.

Finally, the light bulb came on. There was no more putting other people's feelings ahead of mine. It was time I truly start loving and caring about myself.

2007 was an awakening year for me in my life, and I started to see things shift in my life. I became more confident, and more aware of why I was attracting certain things in my life, plus it was starting to be clear to me that I really did have greatness within me. During that year, I was laid off from the job I had in Fort Wayne, and that's when my purpose really started resonating with me. After I got the vision from God, I wasn't sure what I should do with it, so I decided to put the vision on hold because since I was laid off I needed to find a job.

In the summer of 2007, I acquired a job in South Carolina, the change my life needed. I was so sure of myself that every person I met knew that I didn't play, and I was serious with my life and about the love I had for myself. Even the guys I met during that time sensed that they had to come correct with me. I often asked myself, "why wasn't I like this five years ago or five months ago?" I realized that sometimes in life you need to have a test in order to have a testimony. This was that time; my testimony! My WHY! The reason I'm writing this book. I had to go through all those things in my life, for me to be able to tell my story, and maybe the things I was going through would help someone else.

After I moved to South Carolina, God started working on things in my life. My prayer life increase and I was now embracing that there was more to the life than what I thought. Previously, I had to chase love, but when I was in South Carolina, love chased me. I met someone who expressed how much he cared for me. I was not use to all this attention, especially since, I had never experienced it before. As a defense mechanism, I built a wall to protect myself. I didn't want to be hurt again, so that meant he had to work harder to get to know me. I knew that God had placed him in my life for a reason but I just didn't know how to receive him. In my mind, I thought he was trying to run some type of game on me, when in reality he was really just being himself. I also recognized that God had bigger plans for me, and if I didn't identify it soon, then I was going to endure some suffering. We dated for a couple of years and in 2010, he asked me to marry him. This is what's so amazing about God, He allows certain things to happen in your life for you to understand that if you just trust in Him, He will see you through your troubles.

Although I was now married, had a great job, and living the life of my dreams, I always knew that God had a bigger plan for me. I knew that I needed to pray and ask God for some direction. After years of seeking and praying, God finally revealed what he wanted me to do to get my story out millions of people all over the world.

In 2015, God revealed to me the first step in getting my story out to the "millions". I needed to quit my job in order for me to take this initial step. Deep down inside, I was afraid to take this step, because there was a little something in me that was concerned on how bills were going to get paid, and how was I going to get my story out. I also knew that I had to push myself out of my own comfort zone for this plan to flourish like God wanted it. August 28, 2015 was my last day of working in Corporate America.

So here we are today; me writing this book. Me taking control of my life, and my future. My God has really been there for me and although have experienced trials and tribulation, there is nothing like living God's purpose. Now that you have gotten a little glimpse of my life, the next chapters will walk you through the steps I took to find that I am motivated for greatness.

Arletta L. Moore

Chapter 3

Step 1 - Connecting with God

"God is the biggest storyteller, and when we create stories, we connect with him and with each other across cultural, religious and gender boundaries." ~Elif Safak

Have you ever wondered about God? You're not alone. Everyone has come to a point in their lives where they wonder about God — whether He exists, what He's like, and what He wants from them.

Imagine a married couple living under the same roof but never really talking to each other. Unfortunately, it happens, and that cold detachment can describe many people's relationship with God. Think about the last time you had a heart to heart with God, and not just recited the words from a prayer book, but really tapping into the inner core and share the deepest concerns, fears and thanksgiving. In the Holy Bible, it states that you were created for connections. We were created by God to live in relationship with him. *Jesus said, "He who comes to me will never go hungry, and he who believes in me will never be thirsty...and whoever comes to me I will never drive away." John 6:25 KJV*

My Connection with God is what I needed to helped heal my soul. I had been going to church all my life but never really understood the type of relationship I needed to have with God for my life. My lack of knowledge of His love caused me to not appreciate Him regardless of what I've done or what I thought of myself. What I did know is God's presence in my life would produce peace, purpose and power. I knew peace itself was going to produce right relationship with Him, and to myself.

All of this required me to increase my prayer life, and study the Holy Bible. Yes, I had been going to church all my life, because it was a necessity in my mom's home. Even if you partied all night on

Saturday, you have better be up and ready to go to church on Sunday Morning. This was the type of house my mother ran. Unfortunately, throughout years of going to church, I never understood how to connect with God, and I really didn't understand The Bible. I knew I had to pray, but I didn't know how to pray. I knew that I had to pay my tithes, but I didn't know why I had to pay my tithes. I also knew that I had to have a personally connection with Him, I just didn't know where to start. I knew all of this, but was unclear on how it was going to help me in my life personally.

This is when I started to make changes by reading The Bible. I also found a version of the bible that could help me understand what I was reading and how I can apply it my life. Prayer life was the next task I had to incorporate in my life to make a change. As I said earlier, I knew I had to pray, but I didn't know how to pray, so I studied The Bible on prayer. I took the Lord's Prayer and broke it down to levels I could incorporate in my own life. The thing that stuck out the most for me in the Lord's Prayer was, "Thy Kingdom come, thy will be done, on Earth, as it is in Heaven." Thy will be done on earth as it is in Heaven, meant so much to me. Whatever God was performing in heaven; He desire it for me here on earth. That was a high level of encouragement within itself. If great things were happening in heaven, then great things can happen for me on earth. This showed me that God's will shall be done on earth. It also helped me to grow a closer relationship with Him because His will for my life is the same will He has for me in heaven. What an eye opener! This revelation gave me the confidence that God did have a purpose for my life. I just need to go in deep prayer to figure it out. This is when my prayer life increased, and God was revealing a lot to me. Although I was listening to what God was revealing to me, I just had to secure my faith in order to be able to receive it. I knew this was going to take some time and it will be a lifelong lesson that I will have to learn for the years to come. I'm was willing to do the work so that I could reap the reward. My mission was simple increase my prayer life and seek God daily. Yes, I said daily process, not a weekly process, not a monthly process and not even a yearly process. There are too many things that we have to face out here in this world, so a daily checkup with God is a must.

Here's an example of what I'm talking about. In Ephesians 6:10-18 (NLT) The Holy bible talks about putting on the Armor of God, something that you must wear on a daily basis. Here is what the Bible says,

10 A final word: Be strong in the Lord and in his mighty power. 11 Put on all of God's armor so that you will be able to stand firm against all strategies of the devil. 12 For we are not fighting against flesh-and-blood enemies, but against evil rulers and authorities of the unseen world, against mighty powers in this dark world, and against evil spirits in the heavenly place **13** *Therefore, put on every piece of God's armor so you will be able to resist the enemy in the time of evil. Then after the battle you will still be standing firm.* **14** *Stand your ground, putting on the belt of truth and the body armor of God's righteousness.* **15** *For shoes, put on the peace that comes from the Good News so that you will be fully prepared.* **16** *In addition to all of these, hold up the shield of faith to stop the fiery arrows of the devil.* **17** *Put on salvation as your helmet, and take the sword of the Spirit, which is the word of God.* **18** *Pray in the Spirit at all times and on every occasion. Stay alert and be persistent in your prayers for all believers everywhere.* This is why I could not do this process on my own efforts.

As you move from the despair of your past, remember that connecting with God is your first step. God will guide you through the pain, the fear and help you heal your soul. As John 14:21 KJV says,

"*He that hath my commandments, and keepeth them, he it is that loveth me: and he that loveth me shall be loved of my Father, and I will love him, and will manifest myself to him."*

You don't have to be reluctant about your relationship with God. You can be self-assured of God's love for you and His aspiration to bless you. Life in Jesus is gloriously and easygoing. It has one obligation: the obligation of continue to be in union with you. If you stay in union with Him, He'll take care of everything else. When you include this step into your life, staying connected to God is pleasantly effortlessly. You're capable of keeping a vital connection and trust that He will take care of you despite what you had to deal with in the past.

Points of reflection

1. We were created by God to live in relationship with him.
2. God's will for your life will be done on Earth as it is in heaven.

3. You have to put on the whole Armor of God in order to guard your mind of the destruction of the world.

Chapter 4

Step 2 - Dig up the roots

"The roots of all goodness lie in the soil of appreciation for goodness." ~Dalai Lama

People are like trees! Each one of us has the potential to grow into strong tall, mighty creations from God. Sometimes people do not grow into their full potential, because they simple don't know what they are made of. Think about a tree for a moment. All trees start off as a tiny seed and go through growth stages known as seedling, sapling, maturity and old age. No tree can withstand thunderstorms, rain, and wind if it has poor roots. Likewise, in order for you to be GREAT you must be rooted in good soil that nurtures your God – given purpose.

Sometimes we have to ask ourselves What are we rooted in? Are we rooted in abuse, neglect, anger, fear, or lack of self- confidence? If so, this is one of the reasons why we are not moving into our greatness.

We have to be willing to go back to our beginnings. I was just like that moving through life feeling inadequate, unworthy and average. It wasn't until I realized what was keeping me stagnant, stemmed from my childhood. Being raised in an abusive household until I was five years old and later being place in foster care, caused me to develop a distorted view of who I was created to be. However, there was always something inside of me that knew, God had a bigger plan for my life. Just like me, God has a bigger plan for your life as well.

Pluck up the Weeds from your Past

The weeds of your past will grow with you if you refuse to let them go. They will hunt you which will lead you to being stuck in a frustrating cycle of brokenness and misery. The key to plucking up the weeds of your past is to make a choice that a change needs to happen in order to invite God's hope into our lives. I recognized this later in my life, when I was on the verge of taking my own life, for the mere fact that I could not deal with the pain anymore. Let's dig into things I did to start plucking up my own personal weeds.

The first thing I had to do to **transform** those weeds instead of **transferring** it. Here's what I mean, if I didn't find ways to get rid to the weeds of my past, I'll likely be doomed to repeat the mistakes I previously made or transfer the pain onto everyone I interact with. This include my friends, family members, and my coworkers. The same thing applies to you if you don't recognize that you have to transform the pain instead of transferring it. Allow some time to ask God guidance to break the control your past and show what useful lessons you can learn from it, so you can begin moving forward. God is so much more powerful than your history. When you fully trust Him, He will start to transform the weeds into healing and wisdom.

Next, leave the shame of the weeds behind. The weeds of your past can hold a sense of shame that you can carry with you throughout your life. When you silence that voice of shame in your life you can be open to the healing possibility that God has for you. Listen to the Spirit within, that says God loves you totally and completely, despite what has happened or is happening to you. Even though God knows the worst about you, He still wants to redeem you nevertheless. Freeing yourself from the shame helps you accept God's invitation for the healing. This was my biggest breakthrough.

Now let's look at overcoming the regrets that you have with your weeds. When you hold on to the weeds of your past that have produced some disappointments, this only produces more regrets until you break this vicious cycle and release it to God. You have to understand that once you have overcome the fact that you have weeds, then you will realize that it's meaningless to dwell on them, because you can't go back and change your past.

All you can do is moving forward towards your future. Start with a good prayer specifically about each of your regrets and focus on God and not your painful past. You can leave every one of your regrets with God, and this will symbolize that you trust Him and His power.

Your next step is to embrace the weeds of your past. Please understand that you have to accept the reality that what has happened to you in past has caused you stagnation. Don't deny it or minimize it! Take the time to surrender your past to God, and He will take it and use it for good purposes. God always sees you as a first-class person, so express your gratitude to God by following His command to forgive the people who have hurt you. Rely only on His help to do so.

Once you begin to rid yourself of the weeds that have been stunting your growth, you will begin to uncover the true meaning of God's will for your life. When you discover what God has for you, the weeds of the past no longer keep you in bondage. This is what pruning your weeds mean. You have to free yourself from the burden of worrying and align your mind on the decisions that God's will for your life is what will free you from going backwards.

Remember that God has given you the freedom to make your own choices in your life. You don't have to worry about the poor decisions you made years ago or just yesterday. Follow the most loving path of action and trust in God. Trust God to redeem your mistakes and try to make loving decisions from this point on.

Prune Your Mindset

The mind is a creature of habit, so begin to fill up on positive thoughts and eliminate negative ones. You wouldn't allow stinking garbage to build up in your house without taking action. Likewise, don't let negative thinking build up in the inner sanctuary of your mind. Instead clear out the mental heaviness that has weighed you down by pruning your mindset.

According to Webster's dictionary, *pruning means to cut off or remove dead or living parts or branches of (a plant, for example) to improve shape or growth.* The idea of pruning your mindset simple means to rid yourself of any negative thoughts that of you are carrying from your past. When you focus on the lack in your life and believe that nothing will ever get better for you, then you are allowing negativity to control your life.

Furthermore, your mind is the charity of your intellect which really controls your personal self-esteem and drives you to succeed. It is true that sometimes you are faced with some thoughts that you have no control over, but you can actually determine what dwells in your mind and limits your lifestyle. The best way to deal with and forget about your negative experiences is to become fruitful and occupy yourself with productive thinking to produce something positive to impact the world.

When you decide to improve your mind-set and change the way you see yourself, then you can embark on the road to triumph. It does not matter how many times you have been disappointed or failed. Everyone has a past; but you should never allow your negative past to get in the way of your future. It took some time for me to discover this, but I finally realized that the negative images I had in my mind about my history were preventing me becoming all that God wanted me to be.

Emotions like worry, fear, and doubt, are feeling traps that allow the brain to focus on what you don't want in your life. This thought process not only drains your energy but it is very counterproductive to... This is why fear is so damaging and why misery and uselessness must be prevented. So in order to eradicate this negative thinking, you must identify the significance of abolishing them, and be cognizant when negativity is trying to creep your mental space.

Don't think that you can avoid negative thinking forever. Occasionally negative thoughts will ease into you mind. The key is to be diligent in monitoring what you are thinking. Remember that your mind has control over every single action you make — your mind controls your thoughts; your mind tells your body exactly what to do; it tells your mouth what words to speak; it tells your eyes what to look at; it tells your ears what things to pay attention to and what things to tune out; it tells your brain what to think about; and it tells your entire being how to respond in every single situation. That is why it is vital that you renew your mind-set each day with God's word against bad memory, depressive thoughts, and everything that takes your focus off God and places it on you and your problems. You are responsible for the thoughts you think, so start pruning!

Fertilize your gifts

There's a story I heard once about a man and his two large water pots. Every day the man would take two of his empty clay pots and walk down the hill to the river. There he would fill both pots to the top because back home his family needed fresh water for drinking, cooking, cleaning as well as many other things. Both pots were used for carrying water from the river. The pots were the same shape and size but there was one difference between the two clay pots. One of them had a small crack on the upper part of the pot. Even though water would seep through the crack as the man walked back home, the pot remained useful so he refused to throw the pot away.

As he made his way back up the steep hill towards his home, a small but steady trickle of water would fall to the ground to the right of the man's path. For some reason the cracked pot was always carried by the man in his right hand. This scenario played out daily and went on for weeks and even months.

At the same time another scene was playing out. Each day the perfect pot would delight over the fact that the cracked pot was leaking and never brought back as much water to the home of the master. The cracked pot felt so worthless and pretty much had his days of being of any use emotionally numbered. He truly believed that each day when the man arrived home he would finally discard the broken vessel. Each day the man would empty the pots into other vessels for various uses and then place both pots side by side close to his front door.

One day as the man was walking up the steep hill with the water filled pots he noticed the most beautiful flowers lining the path to his right. He could not help but stop to collect some of the beauties and bring them home to his wife. When he gave them to her she was delighted and asked him where he had found such lovely flowers. The man said to her, "My dear, you have this fine cracked pot here to thank for the flowers. All these weeks as I trudged uphill with the pots full of water, our cracked pot kindly watered the path on my right through its cracks. So you see this broken pot is indeed of more value to me than the perfect pot. The cracked pot not only provided us with water but now it has provided us with beauty for our home as well!"

Moral of the story; broken vessels can be the most useful vessels, so don't ever feel that because you are broken or been broken you can never be useful. You have to fertilize your gifts in order for you to understand that you are perfect just the way God made you. The gifts that God has given you are the main reason you were born, but if you don't nurture your gift you will one day diminish your real purpose in life.

EVERYONE HAS A GIFT! You have to realize that your gift was placed within you for a purpose by the Master Potter. Most importantly, your gift was given to you by God's plan and design to be a blessing in someone else's life.

Make it your mission to dig deep within yourself to discover what is holding you back from being motivated for greatness. Your greatness requires nurturing and cultivating on a daily basis, so keep your eyes on the prize. Your roots are what got you here, but your beliefs about yourself are what will keep you here! You can't be your best until you explore the issues that are causing you to be in a state of stagnation.

Points of Reflection

1. Your number one goal to understand that you are motivated for greatness is to love yourself unconditionally.
2. God is so much more powerful than your history. When you fully trust Him, He will start to transform your weeds into healing and wisdom for your life.

3. Everyone has a past; but you should never allow your negative past to get in the way of your future.
4. Your gifts God has given you are the main reason you were born, but if you don't nurture your gifts you will one day diminish your real purpose in life.

Motivated for Greatness

Chapter 5

Step 3 - Get Rid of the Baggage

"It's hard to be clear about who you are when you are carrying around a bunch of baggage from the past. I've learned to let go and move more quickly into the next place." ~Angelina Jolie

Have you ever seen people traveling with so much luggage that it looked like they packed their entire lives in their suitcases? Oh yes, it is a sight to see. It's particularly interesting to see someone attempt to board a plane with more than the airline allows or items that will potentially pose a threat on a flight. Some people become so frustrated because many of their items have to be thrown away. Additionally, in our lives we must be willing to rid ourselves of everything that weighs us down or keeps us from taking flight to reach our greatest level of success!

For so many years I traveled around with mental, physical and emotional baggage. The weight of the baggage was so heavy, it caused me to lose my sense of direction. The garbage that I was carrying around tainted my ability to see the greatness within myself. I wanted to move to higher heights but the weight of my past kept me bound to low living. There was nothing great about that. Have you ever felt that way before? Not anymore. Free yourself of the strongholds that limit you from soaring to new heights.

Unresolved emotional pain can literally kill you. Not letting go of it will eventually make you sick. Laying aside the heaviness will free you from the internal destruction that is affecting your mind, body and soul. It's like a disease that eats away at you physically when it becomes too much to bear. Letting go of the emotional heaviness requires you to accept and express your feelings.

When you can learn to accept that at times bad things will happen, tragedies will occur, people will say and do cruel things to you, just like you will sometimes say and do cruel things to others, then you have taken a huge step forward. Life is packed with experiences that are not pleasant. Acceptance of this is deliverance!

Your next step is to express your feelings. When someone hurts you, forgive them. This is perhaps the greatest mark in your character ... your ability to forgive. Although forgiveness may not be easy, it is still a gift that you give to yourself. But keep in mind that during the forgiveness process remember that everyone is doing the best that they can with what they have learned.

Another thing you can do to lay aside the heaviness of the emotional pain is to live in the present moment. This was an eye opener for me. My mind would always drift to the emotions of the past, but this is what held me back. When I realized that the only moment I had was the present, I was released from my emotional stress. I was able to recognize that if I concentrated on what was currently going on with me, then I didn't have to be haunted by my past, nor be frightened about my future. Understand that living in the moment takes training and diligence.

Stop Taking On Other People's Junk

You are not responsible for other people's junk. This is what I came to understand in my life. There are five dreaded words that most people would say to you in order for you to feel guilt, "You make me feel like...,". What is simply happening here is that someone is making you responsible for their emotional baggage.

This baggage has nothing to do with you. It takes continual experience of being on the other side of taking on other people's junk to get that it is never about you, and always about the other person. I will expound on this further in Chapter 6. Taking on other people's junk only produces familiar feelings of guilt, despair and unhappiness in your because we all share the similar feelings. Some people are more easily triggered by the pain or the unhappiness than others. Discover to honor your own junk first, and it will be a lot easier to allow others to do the same.

No one has ever told you that you must hold on to the weight of the world. Free yourself from the things that are inhibiting you from being the greatest version of yourself. As the songstress, Erykah Badu reminds us, "One day all them bags, gon' get in your way. So pack light!" Let this be your mantra as you push towards mastering your greatness. Leave the mess behind and climb!

Points of Reflection

1. Understand that unresolved pain can kill you, and not letting go of it will eventually make you sick. Lay aside the heaviness will free you from the internal destruction that is affecting your mind, body and soul.

2. You are not responsible for other people's junk.
3. Discover to honor your own junk first, and it will be a lot easier to allow others to do the same.

Chapter 6

Step 4 - Stop the People Pleasing

"Your life isn't yours if you constantly care about what other people think." ~ **Anonymous**

Majority of my life, I wanted to be accepted by being a people pleaser. I've been a people pleaser of the worst kind for most of my life. I tried to make everyone else's happiness more important than mine and I dodged their displeasure at my own expense. Not only was doing this, I created a world where I placed my well-being in the hands of others for them to crumple up like a piece of paper thrown in the trash. I realized that my people-pleasing tactics were just poorly-veiled challenges to sway other people's judgment of and their respond to me.

Although sympathy and kindness are generally seen as positive traits, I naïvely gave from a place of insecurity and low self-esteem in an attempt to bolster my feelings about myself. My problem was not truly loving myself. I was so ingrained in making sure that everyone liked me, and loved me that I forgot to love myself. I thought that if they like me, then I would eventually have their approval of me. This included my girlfriends, guys I dated, and even my family. I never wanted anyone to be upset with me, so I did everything I possibly could to make sure that I please them.

After I started studying the law of attraction, I realized that most of the things in my life that I was experiencing, I attracted it in my life. I didn't understand that you can never fully please everyone and the most important thing that I had to do was to please and love myself. This not only helped me change my thinking, but it also helped me to appreciate that no one is going to make you happy if you are not happy with yourself. I had to make sure that I was the number one person in my life. No thing or person can help me understand that, but me. Once this was clear to me, my life shifted. I understood who I was, and I no longer put my feelings and the things that I want to the side in order to please and comfort others. I'm not saying that I became arrogant, but I just became confident in me. Granted there are still times where I slip back to having low self-esteem or low confidence in myself, but I remind myself not to get into this self-sabotaging phase that I use to do when I was young. I also made sure that God was the head of my life. No matter what I was going through or what answers I needed, I always went into prayer for clarity.

    Remember this, in order for you to meet your own need, and before you can have anything to offer to someone else freely, you have to give and love yourself. Keep in mind that your personal happiness, your relationships, and even your health depends on your ability to reclaim yourself and minimize the people pleasing. This doesn't mean you can never do anything for anyone again, but it does mean you change your motivations and put yourself in the driver's seat of your life. Pleasing others becomes a choice founded in unhealthy self-worth rather than a means to validate yourself.

Points of Reflection

1. Things happen in your life because you have attracted them by your thinking

2. Your personal happiness, your relationships, and your health depends on your ability to reclaim yourself and minimize the people pleasing.

Arletta L. Moore

Chapter 7

Step 5 - Change your mindset

"The very best thing you can do for the whole world is to make the most of yourself." ~**Wallace Wattles**

Your mindset is the totality of your comprehension, including philosophies and views about the world. It is the filter for information you get in and set out. It determines how you obtain and respond to information.

Your mindset is often used for a specific part in your life, like "the mindset of an entrepreneur" or "the growth mindset". Evolving the right mindset is the way of learning something innovative and rid out the most significant information. You can develop the principles that are most supportive for where you want to go or how you want to be. This belief-system is your mindset. You have the ability to change your mindset, so that you can to change your inner beliefs that you base your view of yourselves and the world. However, changing your beliefs is not easy to do. Most people find changing a small belief extremely difficult, let alone a whole range of self-supporting beliefs based on negative pre-conditioning. What is needed is a means – a means for change, that enables you to rapidly install new thought patterns and positive mind-sets. This was the main thing I needed to do in order for me to embrace the full potential of what God had for me in my life.

As I mentioned in the previous chapter, the law of attraction opened up a new world for me. When I discovered the law of attraction, it was the pivotal solution I needed to move to the next stage of my life. The Law of Attraction can be understood by awareness that 'like attracts like'. This means that if we realize it or not, we are all responsible for bringing both positive and negative influences into our lives. The basic part of the Law of Attraction is realizing that what you place your focus can have an intense impact on what happens to you. If you spend your days wallowing in regrets about the past or fears of the future, you will likely see more negativity appearing in your life, but if you look for the silver lining in every experience then you'll soon recognize the positivity surrounding you every single day. For that reason, the Law of Attraction invigorates you to notice that you have the freedom to take full control on how your future develops, and how it shapes the way you see your life.

This was the wakeup call I needed to help me move from self-sabotage to self-acceptances, and know that there was an even more reason that I was motivated for greatness. In 2007 when I was laid off from my job, I had to get out of this major depression state I was experiencing because it was detrimental to my health and my life. I even contemplated suicide. I knew that I didn't want to take my life, but I didn't know how I can move from this self-destruction mentality or the pain I feeling about myself. I wanted to start speaking positive affirmations into my life, so I can change in my thinking and my mind-set. However, I was consumed with the problems of my life and I wanted someone else to feel sorry for me. Then if they felt remorseful for me, they could give me the help I needed. Consequently, instead of me taking the responsibility for my own behavior, I wanted to someone else to take the responsibility, therefore I didn't have to deal with it. This was the worst decision that I could have ever made. My action, my mindset was totally my responsibility, and I didn't want to accept it. Pushing it off to someone else was just setting me back from reaching my full potential.

So the moral of the story… the only way for you to change your mindset is for you to take full responsibility for it. You can't push it off to someone else to fix your problems. You are motivated for greatness and one of the biggest step you need to take to realize that is to change your mindset.

Points of reflection

1. The basic part of the Law of Attraction is realizing that what you place your focus can have an intense impact on what happens to you.

2. The Law of Attraction invigorates you to notice that you have the freedom to take full control on how your future develops, and how it shapes the way you see your life.

3. You are responsibility for change your mindset.

Arletta L. Moore

Chapter 8

Step 6 - Love Yourself More

"Beauty is when you can appreciate yourself. When you love yourself, that's when you're most beautiful."

~Zoe Kravitz

Your number one goal to understand that you are motivated for greatness is to love yourself unconditionally. This starts by getting your body right by exercising. For me, I was not happy with my body, because of the affects it had on my self-esteem. I knew it was important to have a healthy body, because if I didn't feel good on the inside, then how could I feel good about myself on the outside. I learned that exercise would helped me be connected to my body. Once my body was right, I had no choice but to get my mind right. Since the body and the mind are intricately connected, every time I had a thought of self-doubt or self-sabotage, I knew internally how it was affecting my nervous system, which influence all the systems in my body. I also learned that exercise had been shown to have several positive effects on the body. One; it increased the blood flow to the brain by exercise and two; the brain can provide the necessary nutrients such as glucose and oxygen to the body. You may be asking me why am I going into details about scientific significance of exercising, well this is all part of the process of loving myself. You see I had to understand that exercising helped me feel good about myself and how I looked.

Exercise was a must for me so that I can move from self-sabotage to truly loving myself. As I implemented exercise to get my body right, prayer and reading the word was implemented to get my soul right. Studying the Law of Attraction is what I needed to get my mind right. That's when I started to see major changes in my life. Let's start with the body. I went to church for bible study and the pastor was talking about detoxing your body. I thought to myself that this may be the thing I need to get rid of this weight. However, what I didn't know was that detoxing was going to help me get rid of toxins in my body and clear my mind. That year, I started this 10 detox fast called "The Lemonade diet". I was determining to make sure that all that unnecessary weight was released from my body. After completing the 10 days, I felt like a new person. I lost a significant amount of weight, my mind was much clearer, and my confidence was at an all-time high.

Then I start dating myself. This was the pivotal point for me loving myself first. I started going to the movies by myself, taking myself out to dinner, and going to a concert by myself. Once I start doing things by myself and didn't worry about what people thought of me, there was nothing no one could say about me that would send me back to where I was a years ago. Another thing I did to love myself was to set goal. Goals helped me understand that I couldn't just let life happen to me. I must have some intention on my life. The goals set for myself helped me appreciate that I must love myself first before anybody can love me, as I needed to be loved. Now my confidence level was at an all-time high, and I could finally be proud of who I've become, the real me.

In 2008, comedian Katt Williams taught us a very valuable lesson in one of his standups, you must be in tune with your star player. Who is the star player? YOU! This also means you must love your star player. Do what is necessary to keep your focus forward and the wind at your back. Life happens and you have to be prepared to roll with the punches and don't let anything or anyone that tries to stop you from being a superstar and loving your star player. This may include trying something new in your life to change course, just keep in mind that not all will support you in this change. The star player will have to go on anyway. People who you thought were your friends will show who they really are when you are in need. The star player will have to go on anyway. You may lose a job. The star player will have to go on anyway. Sometimes you just have to look in the mirror and get up close and personal with the reflection and have a hard and honest conversation with the star player. The star player is waiting for the team to rally around them to keep going. Sometimes the rally doesn't come, and sometimes you just have to rally around yourself, pick yourself up, let yourself know that you are the best, you are making moves, you don't have time to lay around and be miserable or depressed. You are the star of your life and your team, so start loving that star player. You have to love you first, because if you don't see yourself as a star you, then no one else will either.

Points of reflection

1. Your number one goal to understand that you are motivated for greatness is to love yourself unconditionally.
2. Exercising is a crucial part of loving yourself.

3. Clearing the mind by detoxing to release unnecessary weight.
4. You are the Star player of your life, so start loving yourself as the Star player.

Motivated for Greatness

Chapter 9

Step 7 - Live your Dreams

"The biggest adventure you can take is to live the life of your dreams." ~ **Oprah Winfrey**

You are here on this planet to prosper and live your dreams. The key is first recognizing the process of reality and then choose to take responsibility of your life. This means being conscious of your thoughts, words, and actions and knowingly choose language and a manner that support your accomplishment. Plus, it means putting yourself in a position to receive all the earnest prosperity available to you. Then you can prepare yourself and open the floodgates wide, good things will drift into your life.

The first step in living your dreams is to believe in yourself as much as you believe in your dreams. Too many time people who have dreams fail because they didn't have the self-assurance to see them through. People worry that maybe their dream was too big. They started to think that they weren't actually good enough to want something so amazing. Intentionally know that you are worthy of your dream is the crucial part to bring it to life. Growing up I didn't have the positivity and affirmations to helped create a solid foundation of self-esteem for me.

The second step to living your dream is that you must be okay with failing. If you never try to reach your dreams because you're afraid that you'll fail, then you'll never know for sure if you could have made them come true. I'm sure I'll continue to make mistakes, but one thing that stays true during all of these alleged failures is that I am here today because of them. Each one led to a shift in my perspective and a different path, which led me to the next, and the next.

Next you have to keep going. Over the past

year I have worked for myself, during that time, I had many moments where I wondering if entrepreneurship was worth it. I have examined why did I take this path and if I should just go back to work with the security of a regular paycheck.

But the dreamer in me knew that I had a mission that I had to accomplish. I needed to keep going. I saw so many people in my shoes that kept at it, and I knew that if they keep going despite of the adversity, then I knew I could too. Therefore, I held on and stayed the course, knowing that persistence was the way to success. Staying power and continuing on is what separates the true visionaries and the go-getters from the dream hobbyists.

It's not sufficiently to just have a dream about where you want your life to go and what you want to do. You have to look a little deeper, examine it and choose whether or not it's valuable of devoting your life to pursuing.

Lastly take a risk, and it doesn't mean to do so hastily. People who profit from their risks are the ones who plan for them. They educate themselves on the complete possible of the outcomes and have plans for all possible disappointments.

When you begin taking risks on your dreams you move closer, and that's when you notice the change in your life. The relationships around you will change, and some friends will cheer you on. Nevertheless, there are others who will be filled with jealousy and will keep you for moving forward. Any negative in your life will hold you back from living your dreams so get rid of it. At the end of the day, that's what it takes to make a dream a reality; it takes commitment in the face of everything, it takes thick skin and it takes a work ethic, and it takes risk.

Points of reflection

1. Living your dreams is to believe in yourself as much as you believe in your dreams.

2. Living your dream means you must be okay with failing.
3. Keep going and stayed on course, and know that persistence is the way to success.

Chapter 10

Getting through the rough times

"Sometimes our light goes out, but is blown again into instant flame by an encounter with another human being."
~ Albert Schweitzer

I made the necessary changes, but I had to undo years and years of relying on my own knowledge. Moreover, I had endured so much pain from my past that I needed to give myself a clean slate. The thing about making changes in your life is that it's a process with recommendation in this book that you will never lack motivation again. With every new level in life comes a new devil. Now things were a little more challenging because I had new experiences. Although I started putting myself first by loving myself unconditionally, my new experiences were going to require me to put more of an effort. Yes, I started building a better relationship with God by reading the Bible and praying, but when things got tough, I started to go back to that lack of self-belief. I started doubting God's will for my life. The beautiful thing about God is that he gave us the Holy Spirit. In the previous chapters, I talked about building a closer relationship with God, what I forgot to mention is; I also had an encounter with the Holy Spirit as well.

The Holy Spirit helped me to get back in line with what God's will was for my life. Every time I got off plan, the Holy Spirit would bring me back on the straight and narrow path. This is also the key to evaluate your solutions. Do a heart test and see if what you are doing is still in alignment with God's will, if not, then it's time to do some soul searching and prayer to get you back to God's will and purpose for your life.

Points of reflection

1. When times get rough start building a better relationship with God by reading the Bible and praying

2. With every new level in life comes a new devil.

3. Do a heart test and see if what you are doing is still in alignment with God's will for your life.

Arletta L. Moore

Chapter 11

Time to celebrate your mastery of greatness

"Be not afraid of greatness. Some are born great, some achieve greatness, and others have greatness thrust upon them." ~ **William Shakespeare**

So what exactly is greatness? I believe greatness is the quality that emanates from the inside out. It is who you are when you are honoring your values and living a life of purpose. In other words, when you are stepping into your true Self. What does it mean to have greatness and how to people really get there? Are you born with greatness within you or is greatness made? Is greatness defining as the results of some talent or practice? These are just a few questions that have caused such an intense debate, controversy, and diversity of opinions. The heights of individual accomplishment have always excited us, and for all good reason. Greatness is an important human drive, and without it we would be left with some of our most valuable cultural experience. Greatness truly is letting go of your ego, seeing what is possible and letting it fly. The more you step into what is possible, the more you release those inner voices that tells you what you can and can't do, the more you release your authentic self. By stepping into your power, you create the space to listen to other people into their greatness as well. Therefore, letting go of your ego, letting your greatness fly, only let the people around you to step into their power, their greatness and letting their splendor fly.

Then, imagine if we all created the space for others to be great, we can create possibilities for greatness in everything. What is possible from this place of greatness for everyone? What can we create together when we are no longer come from a place of ego and coming from a place of possibility for others?

Now as for me, yes, I had the tools, but I couldn't fight this battle on my own. It took me years of starting and stopping the process before I understood that I must go into prayer and integrate personal development for me to win in this game called life. Winning is what brought me closer and closer to the will of God, and it can help you as well. This is when you will know that you are Motivated for Greatness....

Points of reflection

1. Greatness truly is letting go of your ego, seeing what is possible and letting it fly.

2. Greatness is an important human drive, and without it we would be left with some of our most valuable cultural experience.

3. letting go of your ego, letting your greatness fly, only let the people around you to step

into their power, their greatness and letting their splendor fly.

Conclusion

There is no easy walk to freedom anywhere, and many of us will have to pass through the valley of the shadow of death again and again before we reach the mountaintop of our desires. ~ Nelson Mandela

We live in a world that takes our life though hills and valley, but please understand that is a part of life. The problem with most people is that when the valley hit, they tend to crumble and don't know how to get back in the swing of things. Because the world is ever so changing, we have to understand that there are also challenges we will face in our lives, so keep in mind that God is here to help you on your journey to Greatness. The steps laid out in this book gives you the guide to go from average to mastering your greatness. Even though it may have been tough for you in the past, please rest assure that your future is even greater than your past.

Finding a solution to what's holding you back from your greatness, it may not be easy, but once you have done the work, it's time to reveal the greatness within you. Your greatness requires some nurturing and cultivating on a daily basis, so keep your eyes on the prize and you will be motivated for greatness.

I would love to hear your story about how you mastered greatness using the steps. Feel free to drop a line or two at arletta.l.moore@gmail.com

For booking inquiries

Contact me at

Arletta L. Moore

(404) 490-1156 or email me at

arletta.l.moore@gmail.com

Please visit my website www.arlettamoore.com for upcoming events and workshops or to learn more about what is going on with me. Take care and thank you for reading Motivated for Greatness. God Bless YOU!

Arletta L. Moore

Made in the USA
Charleston, SC
08 July 2016